WHEN
LOSE
Your
BEST FRIEND

God's Word
for Grieving Pet
Owners

TRICIA KLINE

Tremendous Leadership
PO Box 267 • Boiling Springs, PA 17007
(717) 701 - 8159 • (800) 233 - 2665 • www.TremendousLeadership.com

Tremendous Leadership's titles may be bulk purchased for
business or promotional use or for special sales.
Please contact Tremendous Leadership for more information.

Tremendous Leadership and its logo are trademarks of
Tremendous Leadership. All rights reserved.

ISBN-13 978-1-949033-85-4 (paperback)
ISBN-13 978-1-949033-86-1 (ebook)

DESIGNED & PRINTED IN THE
UNITED STATES OF AMERICA

Endorsements

When You Lose Your Best Friend is simply outstanding in addressing a very important issue with pet-lovers: "How do I handle the grief of the loss?" The book brings insight, understanding, comfort, and spiritual guidance, which is what we always need as we face a loss. The work is woven with scriptural truths bringing eternal perspective to such a loss. The stellar feature of the book is addressing the question, "Will we see our pets again?" The logical path to answering this brings the promise of sustaining hope. The book should be a must read for those who face the loss of their beloved pet.

Dr. Randy Corbin,
former district superintendent of the Christian and Missionary Alliance

When You Lose Your Best Friend was such a comfort to me after recently losing one of my dogs unexpectedly. Tricia writes a down-to-earth, honest guide to managing all the emotions that show themselves before, during, and after the death of a beloved pet. The written memory of her loss sets the gentle tone of her book which goes on to interweave prayers throughout. She addresses questions often thought about when a pet dies but remain unanswered. Grief is not an easy path to walk. The knowledge of not being alone with the sadness brings hope that the feelings of loss will evolve and will be held with love. Tricia's book offers a way of forgiving ourselves for any feelings of guilt. She encourages us to be present with any feeling that may arise and stand in the way of bringing more animals into our hearts.

Kristen Acri
animal advocate and former board president,
Canine Rescue of Central PA

Heartfelt and informative. I could relate to the grieving process having had my own dogs and losing them for various reasons. This book offers an insightful path to navigate through the grieving process using prayer.

Amy Powell,
CPDT (certified pet dog trainer), owner of Doggie U LLC,
Harrisburg, PA

I highly recommend this book to anyone grieving the loss of their beloved animal companion. I believe that the love animals give us is a reflection of our Creator's unconditional love for people. Daily we experience the grief of this loss at our veterinary clinic, and as the Bible says, "Blessed are those who mourn, for they shall be comforted." Thank you, Tricia, for the comfort this book has given me.

Dr. Anne Parker, MVB, Compassion Animal Hospital,
East Berlin, PA

Table of Contents

Dedication

This book is dedicated to friends and family who were there to support me in my times of loss; to all the pets that have enriched my life simply by being a part of it; and to my Heavenly Father who has given all of His creation a beautiful future through the redemption and restoration offered in Jesus Christ.

Introduction

The pet emergency hospital was bustling with activity. It was Saturday, less than two days after our sweet Max had surgery to remove a melon-sized mass along with his spleen. He had developed a slight fever, so we were told to bring him back in for evaluation. Even though he was full of pain meds and tired and obviously feeling miserable, he was still as sweet as ever. He found strength to wag his tail when the workers came to get him and take him back for some testing. He looked back at us a little uncertainly right before he went through the door with them, but he still went obligingly.

We stood in the waiting room for some time. We watched animals and their owners come and go. Some left the hospital with their beloved companion. Some emerged from the back rooms, not only with empty hands, but with gaping holes of loss in their hearts and tears that revealed the deep love they had for their best friend. My heart ached for those people – even before I realized I would be one of them that very same day.

I have had quite a few pets in my life. Growing up, my family always had a dog, each one rescued from the shelter or from the street. We also opened our home to cats, rabbits, guinea pigs, birds, hamsters, and fish. When I got married and we moved into our own home, we continued that tradition of rescuing and loving creatures in need. I even got a hamster from a hamster rescue. (Yes, hamster rescues exist!) I have grieved over many pets, but the loss of Max has felt like the hardest, perhaps because it is the freshest, but also perhaps because of the unique attachment we had with him. My husband and I adopted this sweet, smart, beautiful German shepherd mix three months after we were married. He was a little over a year old. We bonded instantly. I worked mostly from home, so I was with him more than anyone on the planet for nine and a half years. He was so smart and funny, and his pure love for life was contagious. I deal with social anxiety, and Max got me out of the house, interacting with neighbors and going on adventures I never would have taken without him. At home, he kept me in a routine. He kept me moving. He relied on me, and to be honest, I relied on him!

In January, an x-ray and then ultrasound showed a large mass in his spleen. It was a "ticking time bomb" they said. Surgery was necessary to give him a chance. They wouldn't know if it was cancer unless they did surgery and took biopsies. So we opted to give him the surgery, to give him that chance. He pulled through. But following surgery, the surgeon had bad news. Not only did they remove a cantaloupe-sized mass with his spleen, Max's liver was highly abnormal. The surgeon didn't think he would live more than a few weeks to months. Two days later, Max developed a fever, more fluid showed up in his abdomen, and we chose to end his pain. It was the hardest decision we have ever had to make. I mean, how do you choose to end your best friend's life?

When his biopsy results came back a couple of weeks later, we were assured his prognosis had indeed been poor, and that he was probably in more pain than he had shown. But I still nearly suffocated myself in guilt and regret. Nearly seven months later, as I write this, I still cry, I still struggle, I still miss him with all my heart. He and his little chihuahua brother, Howie, who passed in July 2021 at nearly 20 years old (we adopted him when he was 15), were the first dogs for whom I was responsible for making the decision to let them pass peacefully. These decisions left me with a deep heartache that cannot be explained.

No matter how your pet passes – how decisions were made or not made – when they are gone, they truly take a piece of your heart with them.

The fact that you picked up this book means you loved your pet. Your grief is equal to the depth of your love. Your pet knew that you loved him or her, I do not doubt that. I know that won't bring back your beloved furry (or feathered or scaled!) family member. Yet, I hope you can find some solace in knowing that God is pleased with your heart toward His creatures. He dearly loves your pet too. He dearly loves you.

There is little one can say or do to ease grief in times like this. You may doubt you made the right choice. You may have all sorts of regrets. You may be replaying that last day over and over in your mind. Knowing you will never be able to pet them, hug them, or play with them again has created a void that you don't think could ever be filled. You were there for them for every need they had, and now you have been separated. It's hard to imagine the other side of what you are facing right now.

This little book is written from one hurting heart to another. I hope it will steer you to the only comfort I have ever found in these terrible, dark moments. The way I see it, we can turn to anxiety, anger, alcohol, etc. – but all of that just keeps us in the cycle of pain. In the world, we find death. But in our Creator, we find life. God has not only breathed the breath of life into every creature, but He has called every single one of them "good," and I can say with all confidence that He loves every single one of them more than we - their simple earthly caretakers - could ever dare to. That means you are certainly not grieving alone. He will walk with you, as He does with all who are brokenhearted (Psalm 34:18), and if you look to Him, He will give you grace and great hope in the tearful, grief-filled days ahead.

~ Tricia Kline

A Brief Word About Grief

It is unfortunate when grief is considered a weakness, or something to be suppressed. I think that not only stunts healing and hardens hearts but is also a disservice to the loved one now lost.

Barbara Baumgartner once beautifully said, "Grief is a statement – a statement that you loved someone."[1] Queen Elizabeth famously said, "Grief is the price we pay for love." Grief is not weakness. It is strength to embrace loss and enter difficult, emotional, war-torn territory. We step out into a foreign land with no map of the landmarks…or landmines. Yet somehow, we know we must keep walking, because the journey, when we make it through, will make us stronger and bring us to a place of coveted peace, and maybe even some hope.

To prepare for that journey, it is helpful to know the following:

- **Grief is grief.** Some well-meaning (and not-so-well-meaning) people in this world – perhaps you have encountered some – may chide you or attempt to "talk sense" to you for grieving an animal as much as you would a person. Maybe you are wondering if there is something wrong with you for even grieving your pet *more* than you have a person who had been a part of your life. Maybe

[1] In H. Norman Wright, *Experiencing Grief* (Nashville, Tennessee: B&H Publishing Group, 2004), 19.

you hear of others who have experienced the loss of their pet in a more tragic manner, and you're wondering if you should be grieving less than they are. Whatever questions you might be asking about how you should be grieving, let me assure you that there is nothing wrong with what you are feeling. Grief is not something that can be compared with others, because there is not a "right" way to do it. It is less a concrete noun as it is a wide-ranging verb, dependent on the person and their unique connection to the one loved and lost, be that human or animal. According to renowned therapist, professor, and author H. Norman Wright, "The worst loss is your own."[2]

- **Grief has stages, but not a schedule.** Mental health experts have identified varying stages of grief. Some have taught five stages, others seven. But most agree that those stages do not occur in a linear fashion, as a neatly laid out step-by-step grief process. You may return to the intense pain at times and struggle to move forward. It cannot be rushed. And it cannot really be planned.

- **Grief is about rolling with the punches, not ducking from them.** It is human nature to avoid pain. In most instances, that is wise. But grief is unique. If you avoid grieving, the pain only digs deeper. You may want to avoid thinking about the unhappy moments, and sometimes even the happy memories bring tears, because they remind you of what you lost. You may want to avoid looking ahead and learning how to live without your buddy, because that too is just not something you can imagine without great heartache. But to find healing, both are necessary: "Some shut out both past and the

---

[2]Wright, 15

future, but we need both the memories and the hope."[3] The present flees with each passing tick of the clock, but the past and future will always surround us, teach us, and lead us. This is not a journey just to get through, but a journey to embrace. Each step is full of grace-filled lessons – if we're open to learning them. Then, we can anticipate that not only will our situation change, but so will we – for the better. And we will be in a much better position to give our beloved pets the honor that is due them.

[3]Wright, 13

Chapter 1

When the Pain is Too Great to Bear

No matter how your pet passes, it is tragic. Whether a horrible accident, a sudden sickness, or a grueling quality-of-life decision to euthanize, having to let go brings shock and despair. You may have lost your will to go on. Your pet was so much a part of your life that you cannot even begin to imagine how to live without him or her.

I think it is the innocence of animals, their dependence on us, and the gift of their loving, loyal presence, that makes their loss so great. Sometimes the loss is much greater than we could ever fully understand or convey to others, especially those who have never had a pet. We become so emotionally invested in them. They truly become family. For those who do not have children, like myself, there seems to be a deeper kind of pain when the pet we care for is gone. An absence that cuts deep. I have friends, both with and without children, who have told me the loss of their furry family members was one of the most difficult experiences they have ever faced. For those of us who have been blessed to have such a deep bond, the separation is unbearable. The shock may make you feel as though you died along with them.

You may be in a state of grief where you feel lost and numb, and so overwhelmed that it is unthinkable to move – backward or forward – from the present moment. You are stuck, devastated…incapable of dealing with the pain.

Please know that you don't have to have it all figured out. You don't have to try and understand what you're feeling. In this moment, it is not about regaining control, but in simply realizing you are *not* in control.

Let it out

One of the greatest pieces of advice I was given after we said goodbye to Max was to cry as much as I needed to. As soon as we returned home, it also *hit* home. The house felt so empty as I gathered up Max's toys, beds, dishes, and blankets that evening. The tears came like water gushing through a dam. They were coming whether I wanted them to or not. In the following days, there were *a lot* more tears. It was a season that required them.

The wise "Preacher" of Ecclesiastes understood that life would bring all sorts of experiences, feelings, and responses. Wisdom helps us to understand that the seasons on this earth will indeed change. If you are in a season of grieving, then you must embrace that time for what it is: *"There is a time for everything, and a season for every activity under heaven…a time to weep and a time to laugh, a time to mourn and a time to dance…"*[4]

In the midst of our emotions, it is helpful to understand our inability to see beyond them. We may feel that we will never get over the loss or never experience happiness again. Yet there is something inside us that knows there is something more than just this season of life. In this longing, the Preacher looked to God to explain this feeling that we may not, in our limited human minds, be able to fully comprehend: *"He has made everything beautiful in its time. He has also set eternity in the hearts of men; yet they cannot fathom what God has done from beginning*

---

[4]Ecclesiastes 3:1, 4. All biblical passages referenced are in *The Holy Bible: New International Version* (Grand Rapids, Michigan: Zondervan: 1996).

to end."[5] God is transcendent and eternal. He existed before time began and will exist after it. The Preacher understood that the real meaning, and fullness to life, was only to be found in God and His plans and purposes. Yet he still had only a glimpse; he realized even more how limited he was, and how incapable he was of finding meaning in this world on his own.

When you direct your tears to God in this season of crying and mourning, you will connect with something greater than just your momentary heartache (though it seems like it will last forever). Right now, you find yourself in just one aspect of time, one very real experience of this life. But God sees the bigger picture. In fact, He's in charge of it! He loves you enough to meet you in this world of limited time and space. He will love you through this season of darkness. And He will assure you, in your heart of hearts, that this is not all there is. There is something greater to come.

But for now, pour out your broken heart to Him, because that is your present reality, and He is your ultimate strength and hope. It is a time for weeping and a time for mourning. He invites you to let it out.

While he was fighting wicked enemies, David cried out to God because He knew God would listen: *"Record my lament; list my tears on your scroll – are they not in your record?"*[6] In your feeling of defeat by the enemy of grief, God is recording each tear that you cry. Elsewhere in Psalms, the psalmist states, *"You hear, O LORD, the desire of the afflicted; you encourage them, and you listen to their cry…"*[7]

[5]Ecclesiastes 3:11
[6]Psalm 56:8
[7]Psalm 10:17

It is wonderful when we can have people in our lives who offer their shoulder to cry on. They are an important part of the grieving process. You are greatly blessed if you can find those people. But there is none more important than the God of the universe, who not only has power over all things, but takes an interest in you and your needs.

The apostle Peter wrote, *"Cast all your anxiety on him because he cares for you."*[8] Let it out. No matter what time, day or night, He is listening. And He cares.

Let it go

Each day that passed was a struggle. Sleeping and eating were difficult – when I was able to do either at all. Mornings and evenings, in their stillness and time for reflection, were the hardest. Sometimes they still are. It may sound cliché, but we truly do not know how much we've loved until our loved ones are gone.

Grief can be an overwhelming burden that gets heavier when we face it head on. Which is why especially in the days right after the loss, denial can become a coping mechanism. If we were to allow ourselves to feel the full weight of heartache all at once, we would be crushed!

But little by little, if we can release the hurt, we will be able to keep moving forward. God has graciously given us a way to do that.

Jesus came to earth to set us free. Not in a political, temporary way, but in a complete, eternal way. Ever since the sin of Adam and Eve, humankind – and all of creation – has been under the curse that brings pain and heartache. But

[8] 1 Peter 5:7

Jesus, God in flesh, came to end that curse. He became like us, joined us in space and time, to fight the battle that we could never win. He alone, by His grace and love, achieved victory. The writer of Hebrews explains, *"Since the children have flesh and blood, he too shared in their humanity so that by his death he might destroy him who holds the power of death – that is, the devil – and free those who all their lives were held in slavery by their fear of death."*[9]

When Jesus Christ offered Himself as a sacrifice, to die on the cross to atone, or pay for, the sin of mankind, He certainly understood suffering. He was fully God, but also fully man, and He felt the same pain that you and I can feel. Not just the physical pain, but the mental, emotional, and spiritual anguish. In a place called the garden of Gethsemane, the night before His crucifixion at the hands of the Roman authorities, Jesus prayed. He told His disciples who came with Him there, *"My soul is overwhelmed with sorrow to the point of death. Stay here and keep watch with me."*[10] When He prayed to God, He asked if it was at all possible that such a fate, such pain, could be taken away from Him. Yet He submitted to God's will, the will that through His sacrifice, the deep suffering of humanity would find an end.

Centuries earlier, the prophet Isaiah described this coming Savior: *"He was despised and rejected by men, a man of sorrows, and familiar with suffering. Like one from whom men hide their faces he was despised, and we esteemed him not."*[11] Despite the pain he endured for our sake, many rejected Him – and they still do today. But the truth is, *"Surely he took up our infirmities and carried our sorrows…he was pierced for our transgressions, he was crushed for our iniquities; the punishment that brought us peace was upon him, and*

[9]Hebrews 2:14-15
[10]Matthew 26:38
[11]Isaiah 53:3

by his wounds we are healed. We all, like sheep, have gone astray, each of us has turned to his own way; and the LORD has laid on him the iniquity of us all."[12]

Jesus faced grief head on. In His death, He took the punishment we deserved. But that is not all. Jesus rose from the dead. He not only defeated sin; He defeated death. And though we have all been like straying sheep, when we follow Him – our Shepherd – we will find victory over death as well. Not only will we experience that day in the future, when God will fully and finally set all things right, but we can have victory in a daily sense by turning to our Victor, who is able to – and asks to – take our burdens and replace them with peace and hope.

He says to us: *"Come to me, all you who are weary and burdened, and I will give you rest. Take my yoke upon you and learn from me, for I am gentle and humble in heart, and you will find rest for your souls. For my yoke is easy and my burden is light."*[13]

In Jesus's day, "yoke" was used as a metaphor for "obedience, subordination, and servitude."[14] The religious leaders, by and large, were so concerned about obedience to the Law (with little thought to the heart behind it), trying to be righteous and strong in their own efforts. It was wearying to them, and to all who followed their instruction. Here, Jesus declared that He came to reveal God's word and His will. He did not give them more burdens, but rest from those burdens. What Jesus urges is that you follow Him, trust Him, and your soul will find rest. Jesus was echoing a prophecy found centuries earlier in Jeremiah, preached to people who continued to

[12]Isaiah 53:4-6

[13]Matthew 11:28-30

[14]D.C. Allison Jr., *Matthew: Volume 1:1-7*, International Critical Commentary (London: Bloomsbury T&T Clark, 2004), 187-88.

reject the rest that God was promising them. They were trying to handle things on their own, and they were failing miserably. If only they would turn to Him in trust and obedience: *"Stand at the crossroads and look; ask for the ancient paths, ask where the good way is, and walk in it, and you will find rest for your souls. But you said, 'We will not walk in it.'"*[15]

In your grief, you do not need to know it all, figure it all out, and carry everything. The pain is too great for you to bear it on your own. God never asked you to. He simply asks you to obey Him, to follow Jesus. His commandments and His leading bring life, not burdens. His way is best. His way brings rest.

Be rooted in truth

When your pain is too great to bear, and as you learn to lean on Jesus, truth must guide you. The journey of grief is difficult, with lots of emotions – like the twists and turns of a roller coaster that threaten to throw you off track. As you begin to face a new normal, the reality that your beloved pet is no longer with you, you are going to deal with fears, doubts, anger, and sadness. We can easily be taken off course and start believing things that are not true, adding to the burden of grief that we have already been urged to trade for God's rest. Truth is a way to keep us on track, rooted in a right, life-giving response to every feeling that arises from within our broken hearts.

In my own grief journey after the passing of my beloved best friends, I have especially relied on two strong foundational truths to steady me:

[15]Jeremiah 6:16

- **God owns all of the animals. We are only their stewards.**

Everything we have in this life is a loan. Our lives on this earth are so short. The world was turning before we were born, and it will keep on turning after we're gone. But God is both the Creator and Owner of all - including the animals, including your pet.

Psalm 50 offers us a beautiful reminder of this truth. To fully grasp what is being declared there, it is helpful to understand a little about the commonly held religious beliefs of the ancient Near East. Many people believed their gods' images, set in prominence within their temples, had to be carefully cared for and worshiped, or wrath from the god may ensue. Some people believed the gods decided to make humans as a sort of afterthought, so that they could do their menial labor work for them. Animal sacrifices were considered food for the gods. But speaking into this religious milieu, God made it clear that He was the only God, sovereign and not in need of humans for anything! Humans were created simply for His pleasure, the apex of His creation work. And in fact, the only sacrifice ever acceptable to Him was one that was made with a repentant heart, one seeking to live rightly before God (Micah 6:6-8). If it was just an animal sacrifice that He wanted, He wouldn't need humans for that!

> *"I have no need of a bull from your stall or of goats from your pens, for every animal of the forest is mine, and the cattle on a thousand hills. I know every bird in the mountains, and the creatures of the field are mine. If I were hungry I would not tell you, for the world is mine, and all that is in it. Do I eat the flesh of bulls or drink the blood of goats?"*[16]

---

[16]Psalm 50:9-13

Now before you start wondering what this has to do with you and your pet in the 21st century, let me summarize: God made the animals. They belong to Him. As much as you care for your pet, he or she was never actually yours. Yet He loved your pet enough to give him or her to you to be cared for in a special way. And He loved *you* enough to bless you with your pet as well.

We are simply stewards of our pets for the time we – and they – are here. It is important that we treat them in the way God intends: *"A righteous man cares for the needs of his animal, but the kindest acts of the wicked are cruel."*[17] Did you catch that? How we care for God's animals reflects our own character and our own standing before God!

This call to stewardship is also reflected in the creation account of Genesis 1: *"God blessed them and said to them, 'Be fruitful and increase in number; fill the earth and subdue it. Rule over the fish of the sea and the birds of the air and over every living creature that moves on the ground.'"*[18]

That is a great responsibility. Unfortunately, it has been used as an excuse by some to mistreat animals, which we have already seen goes against other parts of God's Word (and His Word does not contradict itself). Authors and scholars Bruce K. Waltke and Cathi J. Fredricks explain that this means humans are to "rule the creation as benevolent kings."[19] Truly, being rulers appointed by God, the one true King, we are to reflect His own care and love for His creation. Regarding humans, one Psalm proclaims, *"You made him ruler over the works of your hands; you put everything under his feet: all flocks and herds, and the beasts*

[17]Proverbs 12:10

[18]Genesis 1:28

[19]Bruce K. Waltke and Cathi J. Fredricks, *Genesis: A Commentary* (Grand Rapids, Michigan: Zondervan, 2001), 67.

of the field, the birds of the air, and the fish of the sea, all that swim the paths of the seas."[20] We take this duty upon us with honor and deep responsibility, knowing that one day, we will give an account to the Creator for either fulfilling or failing that calling.

God wants us to value His creatures. From the start, they were tied so closely to humans. So much so that God brought them to Adam to each receive a special name (Genesis 2:19). He gave you your pet too, to be named and cherished. If you have done that, you have done all that you were required. Sometimes that loving stewardship requires difficult decisions like having to let them go when they are sick. And sometimes we will make mistakes – we are human after all. God just asks us to do our best, with the right heart, and to trust that He is with us, helping us to do what He has called us to do. Their loss naturally leaves us with deep grief. Yet even then we can trust that they are in good hands with their Creator - their true Owner.

• ***God loves His creation, including you and your pet.***
As much as you love your pet, God loves them more. He created them. He created everything, calling each and every object "good" (Genesis 1). Among God's good creation, the animals were uniquely formed from the ground (Genesis 2:19). They were given the breath of life and a steady food source (Genesis 1:30). Read Psalm 104 for a beautiful reminder of God's intimate involvement with creation, including all of the animals.

God gave us Jesus because of His love – not just for a few: *"For God so loved **the world** that he gave his one and only Son, that whoever believes in him shall not perish but have eternal life."*[21]

[20]Psalm 8:6-8
[21]John 3:16

Surely, God's redemption plan has much more far-reaching effects for all of His good creation than we could possibly ever dare to dream. I often think about how He had both the wayward people and the innocent animals in mind when He relented from His plan to judge and destroy wicked Nineveh, giving them added, gracious opportunity to repent: *"Nineveh has more than a hundred and twenty thousand people who cannot tell their right hand from their left, and many cattle as well. Should I not be concerned about that great city?"*[22]

God also rescued the animals along with righteous Noah, and He included the animals in His subsequent covenant: *"I will remember my covenant between me and you and all living creatures of every kind. Never again will the waters become a flood to destroy all life. Whenever the rainbow appears in the clouds, I will see it and remember the everlasting covenant between God and all living creatures of every kind on the earth."*[23]

After rescuing them from slavery in Egypt, God gave the Law to guide the people of Israel as they learned to live as God's people, honoring God as well as one another. But the Law was not just for guidance and protection of the people. He made sure the animals would be properly respected and cared for as well. [24] For example, the people were instructed to keep the Sabbath, a day where they were blessed to experience rest. Rest was the culmination of all of God's work in creation (Genesis 1), and by commemorating that, the people were reminded that "rest" is the greatest good that God desires for His creation. Not fighting to survive, striving to

[22]Jonah 4:11

[23]Genesis 9:15-16

[24]I am indebted to the following for these insights: Roy Gane, *Old Testament Law for Christians: Original context and enduring application* (Grand Rapids, Michigan: Baker Academic: 2017), 306-307.

stay ahead...just resting in God's care, remembering Him for all He has done for us, continues to do, and will do in the future, when struggle – including that with pain and death – will be finally done away with. Under the Law, within the Ten Commandments themselves, animals were also given the same right to rest as humans (Exodus 20:10, Deuteronomy 5:14). Hear also the loving, practical consideration: *"Six days do your work, but on the seventh day do not work, so that your ox and your donkey may rest and the slave born in your household, and the alien as well, may be refreshed."* [25]

In addition, the work animals were allowed to enjoy some of the food they were helping to cultivate (Deuteronomy 25:4), and they were to be equally yoked, pulling uniform weight, so that one of them was not overburdened. Stray and hurt animals were to be helped, and prevention was to be taken to keep them from getting hurt, as well as hurting one another (Exodus 21:1-4, 33-36; Exodus 23:4; Deuteronomy 22:1-4). The Law also considered the wild animals living all around the Israelite encampment. During sabbatical years, when the Israelites rested from cultivation, the wild animals were to be given access to all the food that grew in the fields (Exodus 23:11; Leviticus 25:6-7). The people were instructed to show respect for animal life in other ways as well, such as not boiling a kid in its mother's milk, eating both the mother and baby birds, or slaughtering both a parent and its young from the livestock on the same day (Leviticus 22:28).

The Law also indicates that there is something special about animals that must be honored. The Israelites were instructed to not eat the blood of animals, because the blood represented the animal's life, apart from its meat (Deuteronomy 12:23-25).

[25]Exodus 23:12

Make no mistake. God loves His creation. Even though bad, horrible, heart-wrenching things happen to them in this cursed state, He created them for a reason, and He has never stopped watching over them...or you.

Let your tears fall. They are a gift from God, to lead you to Him. Wright beautifully shared insight from his own grief: "From my own tears I have learned that if you follow your tears, you will find your heart. If you find your heart, you will find what is dear to God. And if you find what is dear to God, you will find the answer to how you should live your life."[26] Tomorrow is another day. Just rest for now in God's loving arms, and let Him be your strength and guide today and in the days to come.

---

[26]H. Norman Wright, *Experiencing Grief* (Nashville, Tennessee: B&H Publishing Group, 2004), 34.

Prayer

Dear Father,

My heart is hurting. The pain is overwhelming. The loss of
_____ has left me broken and empty. I don't
want to even accept that this has happened. I can't even
think about him/her being gone. I'm afraid it will make it
too real, and I don't think I can handle it yet. But I know
you can. I am allowing myself to cry out to you, though I
still don't know what to do or how to fully grasp this horrible
grief. I know you see each tear that I cry, and I will hold on to
the promise that you are able to somehow turn each one into
something good. I know you want to carry me and my burdens and give me rest. Help me to lean on you now and in all
the days ahead. Help me to remember that _____
is yours, and that you love him/her more than I could ever
imagine. Comfort me with your truth. Shield me from the
lies that threaten to keep me in this terrible darkness. Thank
you for offering Light, for both healing and hope. Give me
the ability each day to see it more and more.

In Jesus' Name, Amen.

Chapter 2

When You Feel Angry and Abandoned

Anger, like our tears, is necessary for working through the grieving process. You may be so incredibly tired from feeling empty and lost, and anger may be the only way that you feel alive again. It may be the only way that you feel you can gain a sense of control over the painful circumstances. For a time, it gives you a purpose. You feel you are doing what you need to do to find justice for what seems so unfair: Someone should pay for all of this!

You could be angry at yourself, at others, even at God. All for varying reasons. Angry at yourself or the veterinarian for not doing more to help, perhaps. Angry at the person responsible for the accident that took your best friend away. Angry at God for seemingly not caring enough to act and to save. He could have, you know, but He didn't. Why? Where are you, anyway, God?

You're not alone

If anyone was tempted to believe that God had abandoned him, it was Job. The man was an upstanding citizen who feared God. Yet he had just about everything taken from him – including his health. His well-meaning, yet misdirected "friends" tried to convince Job that surely, he did something to upset God, because He only punishes those who do wrong.

Job, however, knew that could not be the case. He had remained faithful to God. At the same time, he seemed to have understood that God sometimes allows bad things to happen to good people. Good people were never guaranteed a carefree life. When Job's wife urged him to *"Curse God and die!"*[27] Job responded, *"You are talking like a foolish woman. Shall we accept good from God, and not trouble?"*[28]

Though he understood this, Job still struggled to come to terms with the deep grief and pain he was experiencing. He lost all of his animals, his possessions, his children. He was in severe bodily pain day in and day out. He knew his friends were wrong to keep saying that all he had to do was to repent of whatever sin he had committed and God would restore him. Their theology was not consistent with Job's experience. After all, couldn't they see that men known to serve other (false) gods and practice evil things were enjoying their ill-gotten wealth and safety even as they spoke (see Job 12:5-6)? There was another reason, surely, that God was allowing him to suffer. Job looked to a somewhat unlikely source as teachers of this truth:

> *"But ask the animals, and they will teach you, or the birds of the air, and they will tell you; or speak to the earth, and it will teach you, or let the fish of the sea inform you. Which of all these does not know that the hand of the LORD has done this? In his hand is the life of every creature and the breath of all mankind."*[29]

Have you ever considered that your pet had a more unique, I dare say even – in a sense – superior, knowledge of God than you? Animals naturally trust their Creator by way of living in the instinct He gave them. They do not doubt or misinterpret God's Word, as people do. They naturally live in

[27]Job 2:9
[28]Job 2:10
[29]Job 12:7-10

obedience to God's design. They daily experience His sovereignty through His gracious provision.

The last few songs in the book of Psalms create a beautiful crescendo of praise, ending not just with a call for *people* to praise God for his power and greatness, but all of His creatures. The psalmist writes: *"Let everything that has breath praise the LORD."*[30] "Breath" here is a translation of the Hebrew word *nᵉšāmâ* (נְשָׁמָה). The word is used elsewhere in Scripture to describe both men and animals – the life given to them both by God.

The animals do not need to be told to praise God, because they naturally do it. Humans, however, throughout history required written instruction, prophets, psalms like this sung in regular worship gatherings, and eventually God's ultimate revelation of His authority and redemption plan in Jesus, to keep their eyes on their Creator – else they quickly fall into lies and danger. That danger includes believing that God is absent and is not aware, or at least does not care, that you are facing the grief you are now. Or that He was not powerful enough to save your beloved best friend. He is, and He was. You just have to trust Him as much as your pet did.

As fallible humans, who have been given the power to choose, we will have times when we forget that God is with us – in the good as well as the bad. Even David, who was called a man after God's own heart and remembered as Israel's most righteous king, struggled at times – particularly those times when he was in greatest danger or in his deepest depression. In Psalm 31, he praises God for showing his love to him even while he was in a city besieged by his enemies. He admits that he faltered: *"In my alarm I said, 'I am cut off from*

---

[30]Psalm 150:6

your sight!'."[31] But even in his struggle to sense God's nearness, He continued to cry out to Him, and God once again proved He never abandoned him: *"Yet you heard my cry for mercy when I called to you for help."*[32]

God is there, whether you feel Him or not! God is there, even in your pain. Just look at Job. And when you doubt that, just ask the animals.

Keep talking to God

It was a Thursday night. We had gotten a notification earlier that day that a well-respected pet emergency hospital about an hour from our house had a rare opening to perform Max's surgery if we could bring him that evening. We knew every second counted because the mass that was found in his spleen could burst at any time, so we rushed to get everything ready and get there in time. It was difficult to leave him there, but we knew he was in good hands. That evening, as we waited for the phone call to see how things went, I remember sitting on our couch in the living room, my stomach in knots. I silently prayed. *Father, I ask that Max will be okay. I'll still trust you and follow you even if he's not, but if he's not, I might be mad at you for a while."*

It wasn't any sort of ultimatum, as though I was threatening God with the silent treatment. I am fully aware that I do not hold any sort of bargaining power over the Creator and Sustainer of the universe!

What I *was* saying is that if Max wasn't going to be okay, I was going to be angry especially at God because I knew He

[31]Psalm 31:22a
[32]Psalm 31:22b

was the only one ultimately who could save and sustain his life, anyone's life. God's Word and His Way are final. I never once doubted that. But that didn't mean I had to like it if He allowed something I did not want!

Two days later, Max was gone. I wondered where God was, and I was indeed angry (like I warned Him!) that He did not step in to heal him. I honestly wondered if God even cared about me and the fact that my heart felt like it got ripped out of my chest. If He cared, He would have saved Max. Right?

Rather than give God the silent treatment, I knew I had to keep talking to Him. If I had to ask Him those same questions, then I would ask Him. If I had to tell Him I was mad at Him, I would tell Him. He's God. He can take it. He knows everything I'm feeling anyway! And He understood the grief I was feeling and how such grief is expressed. You know what I think? I think He's just happy that we keep talking to Him, even when we do not understand or when things don't work out the way we want them to. Because when we keep those lines of communication open, He's also able to talk to *us* – and I can promise you He will.

When I look back now, I laugh and shake my head in amazement at how God would *not* let me believe for one second that He was absent or that He didn't care. Because I kept reading His Word, even though I didn't feel like it, He spoke to me powerfully through it (be sure to read the next chapter for more on this!). He also spoke to me through others. Now admittedly, I am an introvert and struggle to connect with people and usually prefer to be alone. At the same time, my love language is quality time with people. What can I say? I am complex! But God, who knows me inside out, knew exactly what I needed at that time, and He faithfully and lovingly gave it to me. There is no other explanation for the handful of individuals who said they felt led to continue reaching out to me in those early days and weeks after the loss. One of those individuals reached out before even knowing that I had a dog, much less that he was sick – only that she sensed the Lord was urging us to connect and to simply meet up for a cup of coffee. Each one of these relationships has deepened. Each one shares a great love for animals, particularly dogs, and each one truly understands the difficult journey of love and loss.

God did not save Max, but that did not mean He didn't care. It just means His plan was different from mine.

So many tend to see God as distant and angry, waiting to strike down anyone who says or does something He doesn't like. And therefore, the only time we can approach Him is to ask for mercy from His wrath. This was the common belief among those worshiping various gods in the ancient Near East. But over and over the Bible declares that the one, true God is gracious and compassionate, slow to anger, abounding in love (Psalm 103:8, et. al.). No matter what circumstance we face, we can trust that His love and presence will remain, because He is faithful. Here is our hope: *"For I am convinced that neither death nor life, neither angels nor demons, neither the present nor the future, nor any powers, neither height nor depth, nor anything else in all creation, will be able to separate us from the love of God that is in Christ Jesus our Lord."*[33]

When you find yourself overwhelmed with emotion, even with anger at God and questioning His love, remember to keep talking to Him: *"Do not be anxious about anything, but in everything, by prayer and petition, with thanksgiving, present your requests to God. And the peace of God, which transcends all understanding, will*

[33]Romans 8:38-39

guard your hearts and your minds in Christ Jesus.'[34] In everything, pray. Thank Him for His love, even when you can't feel it. Thank Him for His faithfulness, even when He feels absent. Ask Him every question you have, tell Him whatever is on your mind. When you do this, He *will* respond by giving you peace. Peace that is found only in Him.

He may not give us a reason for having to go through the loss. But truth is, we may not be able to fully understand the reason even if He told us. He is working out all things for good, and when we trust Him, we get to know Him better in the process and learn to hear His voice more clearly. We get to experience a peace that cannot be explained. As Elizabeth Eliot once said: "We are not given explanations, but, to hearts open to receive it, a more precious revelation of our loving Lord."[35]

The root of your anger

Howie, our sweet little chihuahua, was nearly 20 years old and his health was declining rapidly. We made the loving choice to euthanize him, and though it was the right thing to do, it was still incredibly difficult. I had spent several days crying and working through the pain of the loss. And then, almost out of nowhere, I stopped crying from sadness and started crying tears of frustration and anger. I had this growing sense of irritability. I was upset that I was upset! At first, I couldn't figure out just what or who I was angry at. And then it dawned on me. I was mostly angry that such an innocent little creature had to face such an end. It didn't seem

[34]Philippians 4:6-7
[35]In H. Norman Wright, *Experiencing Grief* (Nashville, Tennessee: B&H Publishing Group, 2004), 55.

fair. Why did animals have to die? They didn't do anything wrong!

I think, ultimately, this is the root of all the anger we feel. We may direct it at others. After all, it's easier to blame something or someone you can see. But what we are really angry about is pain and death. We're angry that it has to happen at all. And you know what? We should be.

No one really likes to talk about the sacrificial system that was part of the Law God gave to Israel in the Old Testament. Especially those of us who are animal lovers. It is hard to make sense of the connection between a loving God and the slaughter of innocent animals. But that is exactly the point, isn't it? Innocence lost due to human sin has far-reaching effects, reaching even to the animal kingdom. Sin destroys. On a daily basis it destroys. If left on their own, humankind, in its sinful nature, would become just as it was in the days of Noah: *"The LORD saw how great man's wickedness on the earth had become, and that every inclination of the thoughts of his heart was only evil all the time."*[36] The Flood was actually an act of grace, more than judgment, to end the horrible atrocities that men and women, bent on doing evil, were doing to each other and the rest of God's good creation.

When God began again with righteous Noah and his family, and later with the nation of Israel, the sacrificial system was a daily reminder of the sin that was ever-present in the human heart. The daily shedding of blood reminded them of the curse and served as a way for God to hold back the destruction caused by sin. It curbed, for a time, the torrent of evil that once caused their near extinction.

[36]Genesis 6:5

Animal sacrifice became a symbol of the consequences of corruption, but it also served as a symbolic substitute – a ransom to pay for the sin of humankind. Sin has consequences. Someone must suffer those consequences. God provided the animals – not because He did not value them. He did, and He made it very clear that it was not the death of the animal that pleased Him – rather it was the repentant heart of the person conducting the sacrifice. The animals served such an important role of ensuring that these humans could start again to fulfill their mission of declaring God's love and salvation to the rest of the world. It is that message, after all, that will one day bring full restoration of all creation.

But these sacrifices were only a temporary, feeble substitute. They had to be made over and over because sin was a constant reality. It was a bondage that humans could not break. Only God could. And He did, when he sent Jesus.

In the first century, John the Baptist began the ministry for which God sent him – to call people to repentance and prepare the way for a coming Savior who would finally set people free. One day, when he saw Jesus walking toward him, he made an announcement to the crowd that they would have understood well in their context of daily animal sacrifices: *"Look, the Lamb of God, who takes away the sin of the world!"*[37]

In the cruelest, most gruesome execution, Jesus identified with all the fear and pain we have or could ever experience in this life. That includes the feeling of abandonment. The Scripture tells us that Jesus cried out while suffering on the cross: *"My God, my God, why have you forsaken me?"*[38] His words echo Psalm 22, in which the psalmist also appears

[37]John 1:29
[38]Matthew 27:46

to be suffering and feeling as though God is not present to save. Yet the psalm goes on to show that such feelings are not true, and that though there is suffering now God will achieve ultimate victory: *"For he has not despised or scorned the suffering of the afflicted one; he has not hidden his face from him but has listened to his cry for help."*[39]

Jesus's death was part of God's plan to permanently break the bonds of sin that infected His good creation. Through His death, He put an end to animal sacrifice. And with His resurrection, He secured the hope of future restoration.

God never intended any of the suffering we experience here. Love is only love if it's a choice. Humans rebelled, but *His* love never fails. He remained faithful – calling us back into relationship. He provided instruction for maintaining and honoring that relationship. He provided instruction for how to receive His blessings of forgiveness, renewal, and the hope of eternal life, where there will be no more death, crying, pain, or sickness. No more loss. No more saying goodbye.

[39]Psalm 22:24

Prayer

Dear Father,

I feel so lost and broken, and it seems like you have abandoned me, that you left me to deal with this loss alone. Where are you? Why did you let this happen? Do you even care? Do you even see? Please help me to have eyes of faith to trust what Your Word says, even when I can't see it. It comforts me to know that _____ had a special understanding of your love, presence, and power. Teach me to praise and honor you in all things, just as the animals do. Help me to remember, or see, times in the past when you showed your care and faithfulness, and to trust that you will again. Give me strength and the words to keep talking to you. Give me ears to hear your response, however you graciously choose to speak. Help me to keep a right focus for my anger. We all suffer because of sin. Make my heart continually repentant, yet also continually thankful that you sent Jesus to release the power of sin and death over me, and the world. Comfort me in my heart of hearts, with the truth of a brighter future. For those who put their faith and trust in Christ, there are greater things in store than we could ever imagine.

In Jesus' Name, Amen.

Chapter 3

When You Can't Shake the "What ifs"

Time. Before a loss, we want more of it. After the loss, we want to go back.

Time. We are forever caught within its snare. It keeps moving, giving no heed to our desires, our suffering, or those of our loved ones.

For those who must make the heart-wrenching decision to euthanize a pet, the so-called "bargaining" stage of grief can begin before the loss. You attempt to make deals with God, promising to be a better person in some way if only your buddy would be spared. Somehow, you find a way to lay the trouble on yourself, burdening your already drooping shoulders. You long to go back in time. Hindsight is 20/20. If only you knew earlier. If only you had another chance.

The same goes for those who have lost their pet in a tragic accident, or who never found a pet that ran away. You may act as though the accident was your fault, and you replay over and over in your mind the incident and what you could have done differently. No matter how your pet is lost, you may live with such unbearable guilt that the only way you feel you can cope is to stay in the past, before the decision was made, the sickness struck, or the accident happened. You may feel as though the story could change somehow if you replay it again, and this would all just be a dream. Or maybe you will see something this time that might take away the suffocating pain and heartache.

Calming the chaos

I think I was somewhat prepared for the pain and the tears. It was the guilt and the questioning that was the most unexpected and the most suffocating. Did we let Max go too soon? Did we follow the veterinarian's recommendation too quickly? Was there some other way we could have helped him? Did we do the right thing? What if we had discovered his sickness sooner?

I cannot tell you how many times I replayed those questions and the scenario, particularly his last few days, over and over in my mind. I felt responsible. I cared for his every need for more than nine years. And then just like that, I could not help him anymore. I felt like I betrayed him. What if I had done something differently – would he still be here? Would he have been okay?

When it's your best friend, you never, ever want to say goodbye. Love puts us in a difficult place. Do we let them suffer so we don't have to enter the searing pain of loss? Or do we let them go so they can be freed from sickness and pain?

When we received Max's biopsy results two weeks later, the doctor who called said his prognosis had been poor and that we did the loving thing by letting him go. But even then, I still wondered. I still doubted. The guilt would have eaten me alive, had God not spoken to me so clearly. He gave me something to hold on to – an anchor for every time those thoughts threatened to stir up the waves and throw me overboard.

Appropriately, God directed me to a biblical account about some frightened, storm-tossed individuals.

The day after we lost Max, we were really hurting. It was a Sunday. We stayed home to grieve. The last thing we wanted was to be around people. It was the first morning

without Max there to greet us. I didn't feel like doing anything, honestly. But in an attempt to keep some sort of routine, I opened my Bible. I read through the Bible every year
and follow a planned reading schedule. That day's scheduled
reading included Matthew 14. The chapter describes Jesus
feeding the five thousand, then sending His disciples into a
boat to go to the other side of the lake while He stays behind
to pray. Meanwhile, the disciples get caught in a storm, and
the boat – now far from shore – gets hammered by the tem-
pestuous wind and waves. In the early morning hours, Jesus
comes walking on the water toward them! Their first thought
wasn't that it was Jesus, but a ghost. And they were afraid!
But Jesus immediately responds, *"Take courage! It is I. Don't be
afraid."*[40] Then Peter calls out, wanting to know if it was really
Jesus: *"Lord, if it's you...tell me to come to you on the water."*[41] Jesus
does. He tells him to come. And Peter gets out of the boat
and walks on the water toward Jesus! But then he saw the
wind, became afraid, and began to sink. All he could do was
cry out, *"Lord, save me!"*[42]

Jesus catches him before he goes under. Then He had
some simple, yet powerful words for Peter: *"You of little faith...
why did you doubt?"*[43]

It's a compelling story. But I didn't think too much of it.
I think I was too much in a daze of grief to focus on anything
else. Reading the Bible and praying seemed little more than
going through the motions. God felt distant. I was angry, con-
fused, and so very sad.

[40]Matthew 14:27
[41]Matthew 14:28
[42]Matthew 14:30
[43]Matthew 14:31

Later, we turned on a live feed of a church service. It was something to at least get our minds focused on something else. The sermon that day? It was on Matthew 14. The same story of Jesus walking on water, of the fear of the disciples, of Peter's struggle to maintain faith, of Jesus' salvation and patience toward Peter's doubting.

Interesting coincidence, I thought.

Later, my husband Justin was reading his scheduled devotions for the day. He shared a portion of it. Once again: Matthew 14. The same story of Jesus walking on water, of the fear of the disciples, of Peter's struggle to maintain faith, and Jesus's salvation and patience toward Peter's doubting.

At this point, I was starting to think that maybe it wasn't a coincidence after all. Could God be saying something to me, to us?

Later that evening, I decided to distract myself by catching up on the emails that had accumulated over the previous days of chaos and heartache. One of the emails was from a dear faith-filled woman who several years earlier had added me to her list to receive encouragements that she sent out several times a week. Sometimes they were links to videos, sometimes a story, sometimes just an encouraging Scripture verse. There in my inbox was a simple photo of a shoreline being battered by waves and containing a Scripture.

"Take courage! It is I. Don't be afraid. Come. You of little faith, why did you doubt?"

The words of Jesus found in Matthew 14.

He finally had my attention. The tears came when I finally realized this was no coincidence. God saw me. He was speaking to me. What did He want me to know from this passage?

In the weeks that followed, I spent a lot of time thinking about that account. I listened to sermons on it, read commentaries about it. I reread that passage so many times. Over and over again, I discovered fresh insights from those few little verses that spoke to my situation. Here are a few things that I considered:

- God is with me, even in the storm – and even when I, like the disciples, do not recognize Him and am full of fear.
- Jesus told His disciples to get in the boat, knowing they would get caught in that storm. Could our difficult experiences be part of God's greater plan to reveal Himself to us?
- Peter had at least some faith that the impossible was possible with Christ. But he struggled to maintain that faith when he had absolutely no control over his situation. Is my faith only as strong as my grip on the side of the boat?
- Even though his faith faltered, in his desperation, Peter still knew where to turn. Jesus did not refuse to save him because he struggled to have faith. His grace is greater than our failing; otherwise, it wouldn't be grace!
- I must keep my eyes on Jesus, not on myself or the difficulty.
- I must not doubt that God is in control of all things, and nothing happens without Him noticing. I was reminded by a sweet friend, who had been praying with me during Max's sickness, that God had answered our prayers. We prayed that he would receive quality care, and that God would help us make the right decisions for him. I had also been praying that God would sustain Max and keep that large mass (of whatever it was!) from bursting. The surgeon confirmed this when he expressed his shock at how big that hematoma was, and that it never burst (and this man has done this particular surgery numerous times). I believe that was God sustaining Max and giving us time to say goodbye to him peacefully.

At the end of this account, Jesus and Peter climbed into the boat, and the wind died down. The storm was no longer tossing them about. The presence of Jesus, who had defied natural science and walked on water, who had enabled Peter to walk on water, now calmed the sea. The disciples that day, if they had not understood it before, knew for sure that Jesus was the Son of God. No one else could accomplish what He just did.

A common belief in the ancient Near East and the Greco-Roman religions of the first century was that water represented chaos that had to be controlled. Stories abounded of how the many gods of the pantheon had fought to control the sea. Their creation accounts consisted of gods who fought with one another to have control over the watery abyss to confine it and establish the land and sky. It was utter chaos of defeating, killing, and cheating as the gods each sought to establish their authority over the others. In some early mythologies, the gods were the personification of the natural forces, and humans were constantly making sacrifices or practicing magic in the hopes that the gods would protect and provide for them.

The Bible's account of creation is quite different, however. There, God acts alone. He creates for the joy of creating, out of love of His creation. He had no need to struggle over the watery chaos, because He existed before it and apart from it. He is not just one actor in a pantheon of gods. He is the only God. He did not have to fight to create. He had only to speak, and it was so. His word was final, and full of love, and He graciously made it known to us so that we did not have to wonder in vain.

Jesus was God in flesh. In Matthew 14, He walked on the waves. They did not threaten Him. A few chapters before this, Matthew writes of another encounter that Jesus had with tempest-tossed waters. While in a boat with His disciples, a storm suddenly comes upon them, and waves threatened to drown them all. What is Jesus doing? Sleeping. What are His disciples doing? Frantically trying to wake Him, to tell Him they were going to drown and they need Him to save them. Jesus speaks similar words to them, as He spoke to Peter: *"You of little faith, why are you so afraid?"*[44] He proceeded to calmly stand up and rebuke the wind and waves. And simple as that, the storm stopped. Matthew describes the disciples' response: *"What kind of man is this? Even the winds and the waves obey him!"*[45]

One word, just His presence, calms the chaos. Why did Peter ever doubt? Why do we?

If God has control over the most dangerous forces of nature, can we really think that He was not in control of the events surrounding our pet's passing?

Peace in Providence

If amid the storm Jesus walked on the water and rescued the struggling Peter even when his faith faltered, how could we ever believe that God does not see us, or does not care? Jesus' very coming to earth, to die on our behalf and set us free, decimates such a thought. And His words about a common – and extremely disliked – little bird, confirm it.

During Jesus's earthly ministry, He sent His twelve disciples out to do His work of driving out evil spirits and healing diseases and sickness. But first, He gave them some warnings and instructions. First, they should be prepared to be hated and persecuted by the very people they were going out to

[44]Matthew 8:26
[45]Matthew 8:27

help. The disciples were identified with Christ, and many people did not want to hear the message Christ came to bring – repentance in preparation for God's coming Kingdom. But even so, they needed to share the truth and reach out to help even those who would hurt them. As they did, God would go with them, empowering them body and soul to fulfill their mission. In a sense, they were invincible – nothing could happen to them unless God allowed it to. They needed only to trust and obey.

Jesus told them this was true even for the lowliest of creatures:

> *"Are not two sparrows sold for a penny? Yet not one of them will fall to the ground apart from the will of your Father. And even the very hairs of your head are all numbered. So don't be afraid; you are worth more than many sparrows."*[46]

In that day, sparrows were nothing more than cheap food and hated pests. They were extremely common and multiplied quickly. They lived close to humans and often stole food from them. Not only were they irritating to humans, they were also the bane of other birds' existence, often aggressive and pushing them out of an area.[47]

If a single, lowly, even despised, sparrow was in God's view and could not fall unless He allowed it to, your pet could not have passed apart from His providence either. I encourage you, as you face the "what-ifs" of your situation, to find peace in the sovereign rule and compassion of our Creator. Do not fret. The world does not rest on your shoulders, but on His. He alone can handle it, and He alone does all things well.

[46]Matthew 10:29-31; see also Luke 12:6-7
[47]See Debbie Blue, *Consider the Birds: A Provocative Guide to Birds of the Bible* (Nashville, Tennessee: Abingdon Press, 2013), 87-88.

A special bond

David had humble beginnings as a shepherd of his family's sheep. It wasn't a glorious profession, but pastoralism in that region was extremely necessary for survival. The livestock depended on people, and people depended on the animals. As a shepherd, David would have spent most of his time out in a lonely field with nothing but the sheep. He was tasked with ensuring they had enough to eat, water to drink, and that they would be protected from enemies. He testified himself that he had saved his flock from both lions and bears, with the Lord's help (1 Samuel 17:34-37). The experience taught him to care, to fight, and to lead, and he would eventually carry that into his role as King of Israel. The sheep, in their innocence and vulnerability, needed his help. He no doubt formed a special bond with them.

Perhaps this is why he became so upset when the prophet Nathan approached him and told him a tragic story about a man and his beloved little lamb.

"There were two men in a certain town, one rich and the other poor. The rich man had a very large number of sheep and cattle, but the poor man had nothing except one little ewe lamb he had bought. He raised it, and it grew up with him and his children. It shared his food, drank from his cup and even slept in his arms. It was like a daughter to him. Now a traveler came to the rich man, but the rich man refrained from taking one of his own sheep or cattle to prepare a meal for the traveler who had come to him. Instead, he took the ewe lamb that belonged to the poor man and prepared it for the one who had come to him."[48]

We animal lovers can identify with David's fuming anger at the rich man's heartless lack of pity. David immediately shouted that the man deserved to die (2 Samuel 12:5)! He

[48]2 Samuel 12:1-4

then demanded, at the very least, justice for the poor man. David immediately passed judgment on the rich man according to the Law. While recognizing the rich man's callousness, David was full of pity for the poor man's loss. He was mad, and rightly so.

Nathan's story certainly got David's attention. Now, it is true that David would learn that the story was God's way of convicting him for committing adultery with Bathsheba and then having Bathsheba's husband Uriah murdered. David was the rich man in Nathan's story. As king, he had everything he could ever want or need, but he decided to take Uriah's beloved wife instead. Whether it is Uriah and Bathsheba, or the poor man and his beloved ewe lamb, a conclusion can be drawn here that God sees injustice and cherishes pure, committed, loving bonds. That includes the bonds we have with our pets.

Psalms 32 and 51 give us a glimpse into David's heart. Though he sinned, committing terrible injustice, he was repentant and longed to be restored to God and to live righteously before Him and his fellow man. In perhaps his most famous psalm, Psalm 23, he beautifully depicts what an unhindered bond with God looks like. And not surprisingly, the picture is one of a little lamb and his owner.

"The LORD is my shepherd, I shall not be in want."

The Lord cares for David as a good shepherd cares for his lamb.

"He makes me lie down in green pastures, he leads me beside quiet waters, he restores my soul."

Whenever David was in need, going the wrong way, or facing dangerous circumstances, his Shepherd was lovingly there to guide him.

"He guides me in paths of righteousness for his name's sake. Even though I walk through the valley of the shadow of death, I will fear no evil, for you are with me; your rod and your staff, they comfort me."

This Shepherd goes beyond just being present and protecting his lamb, however. He also pours out abundant blessings and promises that those blessings will never end.

"You prepare a table before me in the presence of my enemies. You anoint my head with oil; my cup overflows. Surely goodness and love will follow me all the days of my life, and I will dwell in the house of the LORD forever."

Perhaps David was thinking of that little lamb in the story. The lamb that lived in his owner's house and was so dearly loved. Only with the LORD as *his* Shepherd, no wicked person would pose a threat. This loving bond in God's presence would last forever, in God's house.

In God's house, all creatures – including your pet (and the unloved sparrow!) – find a home, full of love and life. This is why the psalmists celebrated the incomparable blessing of being God's beloved children, able to dwell with God:

"How lovely is your dwelling place, O LORD Almighty! My soul yearns, even faints, for the courts of the LORD; my heart and my flesh cry out for the living God. Even the sparrow has found a home, and the swallow a nest for herself, where she may have her young – a place near your altar, O LORD Almighty, my King and my God. Blessed are those who dwell in your house; they are ever praising you."[49]

God understands the love and connection you had for your pet. No matter how you lost your best friend, He understands the pain of separation. He longs to form a bond with *us* that

[49]Psalm 84:1-4

daily reminds us of His desire for us to live in His protective care. He wants you to know that He will walk with you through every pain and loss that this life can bring.

He sees you as His beloved lamb whom He longs to care for and protect. He does not want you to dwell with the crippling guilt and "what-ifs" of your beloved pet's passing. You are not the shepherd. You are a sheep. He wants you to trust Him that even in this dark time He is in control of all things, and there is no need to fear or want for anything as long as He is watching over you – as long as you have found a place in His house.

Prayer

Dear Father,

I can't seem to stop replaying in my mind the time around
_____'s passing. I can't stop wondering if things
would have been different had I done something different.
The guilt is overwhelming, and it feels like I will have to live
with it forever. Will you calm this chaos like you did the sea?
I cannot control the wind and waves that are threatening to
pull me under, but I know you can. Help me to remember
my place as a sheep, and you alone as the Shepherd who
cares so much for your flock. Help me to remember that
your loving care and notice reaches to every creature, including _____. Nothing, no one, dies apart from
your will. I struggle with the 'what-ifs', but help me to dwell
instead on the 'what is' – that you are in complete control,
that all life is in your hands, and that you have a plan. I may
not fully understand your plan, but help me to trust that it is
good, because *you* are good. Thank you for the bond I had
with _____. Thank you that you seek to have an
unbreakable bond with me, and with all of your creation.
Thank you for the promise that, as your sheep, we do not
have to struggle and strive and doubt, but we can find a safe
place in your house forever.

In Jesus' Name, Amen.

Chapter 4

When the Sadness Sets In

About eight years ago, my parents rescued a sweet mutt named Maya. She was three years old. She was part beagle and most likely a smattering of various other breeds – possibly a pointer, a lab, maybe even a Doberman! We may not have known *what* she was, but this girl made sure we knew *who* she was. She had a sweet and spunky personality. She never turned down a rub, a hug, or the opportunity to beg for (or steal!) a treat. Toward the end of her life, she seemed to slow down a bit. We chalked it up to old age. That might have been part of the story, but it wasn't all of it.

Little did we know that a deadly tumor was growing inside of her. One day last November, she was her normal self in the morning, then in the evening, she collapsed. My parents rushed her to the pet emergency hospital, where it was determined the tumor had burst. She subsequently suffered cardiac arrest, and they had to make the decision to euthanize her. My parents said the suddenness of the loss was heartbreaking and difficult to come to terms with. When the shock wore off, the realization that Maya was gone began to set in. It was the finality of it all that was hardest to grasp.

Often, when our minds and hearts have learned to work through the pain, the anger, and the guilt, the loss becomes less like a short, intense battle and more like a long, grueling war. Depression becomes almost like a new normal. A deep sadness becomes our new state of existence, at least for a while.

It's okay to be sad

As much as our society speaks about depression, it still seems to be so misunderstood. The default over the past several decades has been to attribute depression to a chemical imbalance – a clinical condition that can be treated with medication or a psychologist. That notion has been challenged more recently as the physical and emotional complexities of depression are being studied more closely, but it is understandable why it was embraced for so long. No one wants to be depressed, and if it can be controlled by a simple pill, why not?! Sadness and hopelessness have been behind many a suicide, broken relationships, and addictions of all kinds. Depression is something to be covered up – eliminated.

But what if depression is something to be embraced? Perhaps in our rush to avoid the struggle, we have failed to see its usefulness, its greater purpose. I believe depression is not an end; it is a pathway to a new and better beginning.

In Romans 8, the apostle Paul indicates that *all* of creation is suffering under the effects of mankind's sin and longs for the day when those sufferings – the decay it experiences daily – will end. The promise of liberation to those who follow Christ is thus extended to the non-human world, which equally fell under the universal curse yet did not play a part in the choice to sin.

I remember especially dwelling on this Scripture when our family lost our pygmy goat, Zacchaeus. I use the term "pygmy" loosely, because that once adorable little baby goat quickly ballooned into an 80-100-pound adolescent with huge horns and big personality to match. He and I had a love-hate relationship. I think he must have seen me as a sibling to play rough with, because every time he saw me, he'd come running across the yard to buck me with those horns. He was a lot calmer with my mom; I don't know if it was her ability to take control (a skill she probably learned while raising five human kids!), but he quickly became "hers." Zac lived in a fenced-in pen with a large wooden playhouse for a shelter. My mom would regularly take him out for a walk around the yard and tie him out front for fresh grass and a change in scenery. He learned to open his own gate with his mouth and to open the shed door with his horn so he could help himself to his hay and food. He was smart and destructive, so he had to be watched closely!

Several years later, we noticed him starting to slow down. There were times when he did not want to eat – which was definitely out of character. One week, when my parents were traveling, I stayed home to house- and pet-sit. Zac took a turn for the worse. I remember going out to check on him. He was lying in his house, his "baaa" to greet me faint and muffled. He refused to eat. He just looked at me with sad eyes. I no longer saw in his eyes that mischievous spirit of his, but an innocence afflicted with the earthly reality of pain and sickness. A farm animal vet was called to the house, and we lovingly, peacefully, ended his misery.

Truly, *all* of creation groans for a better existence. As Paul wrote: *"We know that the whole creation has been groaning as in the pains of childbirth, right up to the present time."*[50] The image used here is important. It is not speaking of the pain of death, but of the pain of childbirth. While the labor process is painful, it ends with new life.[51] Paul goes on to say that Christians, having received the Holy Spirit, also *"groan inwardly as we wait*

[50]Romans 8:22
[51]Leon Morris, *The Epistle to the Romans* (Grand Rapids, Michigan: William B. Eerdmans Publishing Company, 1988), 323.

eagerly for our adoption as sons, the redemption of our bodies."[52] The Holy Spirit is a gift that gives us a beautiful glimpse of what is to come. It is our connection to Heaven, and makes us long for this hope even more. That hope gives us strength to endure these momentary, present sufferings that we experience on earth.

Paul refers to a Christian's status as "sonship." Once we trust in Christ for salvation, we become God's children, guaranteed of a future liberation from the pain of this world. But we have not yet been officially "adopted" until we are at home with God – and that is what we long for most of all. While we await that day, however, we experience weakness and lack of faith. Life is hard; loss is harder. We often get lost and don't know what to say or where to turn. Morris writes, "We are weak, and left to ourselves we will always be in trouble."[53]

This, again, is the blessing of the Holy Spirit for those who have received Him. Paul writes that as we groan for something better, the Spirit groans with us, but *"with groans that words cannot express."*[54] The Spirit takes our inability to know or express our deepest need and translates our groans into a prayer before God that aligns perfectly with God's will. And we know that all prayers according to God's will are always answered and are for our ultimate good (Romans 8:28).

Jesus Himself gave us a promise of blessing for those who mourn. In his famous Sermon on the Mount, he stated, *"Blessed are those who mourn, for they will be comforted."*[55] The Greek word translated here as "mourn" is *pentheō*. Nearly every time the word is used in the New Testament, it is in

[52]Romans 8:23
[53]Morris, 326
[54]Romans 8:26
[55]Matthew 5:4

conjunction with the words "weeping" or "wailing", and usually within the context of a response to death, loss, or sorrow. While grief is the inward feeling, mourning is the outward manifestation of it. By God's design, mourning allows us an avenue for healing.

A dear friend and spiritual mentor, John Fogal, wrote a beautiful work on the Beatitudes included in Jesus's Sermon on the Mount. In his chapter on this beatitude about "mourning," he wrote: "When pain is pent up inside, it can poison the mental and emotional and spiritual system. Conversely, mourning leads to the cleansing of that poison."[56] There is a path from pain to joy – a concept also relayed by Jesus in His parting words to His disciples. Jesus knew He was about to die, something that His disciples would of course mourn. But their mourning would not last forever. Jesus, like Paul, used the image of childbirth: *"A woman giving birth to a child has pain because her time has come; but when her baby is born she forgets the anguish because of her joy that a child is born into the world. So with you: Now is your time of grief, but I will see you again and you will rejoice, and no one will take away your joy."*[57]

Because Jesus rose from the dead and promised to come again for his people, the present grief could be endured because of the assurance of future joy. Jesus also promised them that they would not be left alone until that time. Again, the Holy Spirit is their strength and guide, and ours, as we finish the purpose to which we are called here on earth: *"... the Counselor, the Holy Spirit, whom the Father will send in my name,*

---

[56]John W. Fogal Sr., *Living the Beatitudes: See how you are being conformed to the image of Christ* (ChurchSmart Resources, 2013), 72.
[57]John 16:21-22

will teach you all things and will remind you of everything I have said to you.[58]

Then, coming on the heels of this promise from Jesus is another beautiful one: *"Peace I leave with you; my peace I give you. I do not give to you as the world gives. Do not let your hearts be troubled and do not be afraid."*[59]

When we grieve deeply, we must allow ourselves to mourn. We mourn most of all over the sin that has caused the pain and loss that we experience in this life. But when we do that, we experience cleansing forgiveness, and we become a new creation with ears to hear God's voice and to see glimpses of a perfect, eternal future with Him. Truly, those who mourn are blessed, because *"they will be comforted."*

God does not change

When you feel depressed, it is hard enough to get out of bed every day, yet the world keeps spinning and your responsibilities continue. It is hard to find a steady footing amid grief when everything keeps moving and changing. The weakness we experience in our sadness is heavy enough. We certainly don't want to add worry or doubt to the load!

I believe this is why Scripture is so unequivocally clear about God's unchanging nature. It is a great comfort for those who have put their hope in Him.

This, in fact, was one of the most unique characteristics that God revealed about Himself to His people in the Old Testament. Such a concept was foreign when compared to the other "gods" of the surrounding nations, whose feelings were constantly changing. This left their worshipers to constantly

[58]John 14:26
[59]John 14:27

worry about angering them in some way or being at the receiving end of wrath on any particular day, for no particular reason!

When God spoke through the prophet Malachi, it was nothing short of a polemic against these "gods" and a firm reminder to His people that He was not capricious; He was always true to His unchanging Word.

"I the LORD do not change…"[60]

He never leaves His people without a clear revelation of who He is or what He expects. He has never reneged on any promise He gave, and He never will. He does not change, even though we, and our circumstances, do.

The New Testament repeats this truth when speaking of Jesus: *"Jesus Christ is the same yesterday and today and forever."*[61] This statement comes at the end of a letter written specifically to encourage Christian believers to persevere in the face of extreme difficulty. There is no strength, no purpose, no hope without faith in the unchanging God.

One of the Bible's most powerful, repeated metaphors is of God as a rock.

"The LORD is my rock, my fortress and my deliverer; my God is my rock, in whom I take refuge."[62]

This is why we can come to Him for anything, anytime, anywhere.

"Hear my cry, O God; listen to my prayer. From the ends of the earth I call to you, I call as my heart grows faint; lead me to the rock that is higher than I. For you have been my refuge, a strong tower against the foe."[63]

[60]Malachi 3:6
[61]Hebrews 13:8
[62]Psalm 18:2
[63]Psalm 61:1-3

God will comfort, protect, and provide

That same psalm describes the refuge offered by God with another encouraging metaphor:

> *"I long to dwell in your tent forever and take refuge in the shelter of your wings."*[64]

My prayer is that we all learn to see God this way. His deepest desire is that we trust Him, depend on Him, rely wholeheartedly on His love that can carry us through our greatest depression. Unfortunately, throughout history, so many have failed to do this and have suffered the consequences. In a similar metaphor as the above psalm, Jesus grieved over the state of the people of Jerusalem who had wandered so far from God's ways and His loving provision:

> *"O Jerusalem, Jerusalem, you who kill the prophets and stone those sent to you, how often I have longed to gather your children together, as a hen gathers her chicks under her wings, but you were not willing."*[65]

Other than our family's attempt to raise a couple of leftover chicks from a fifth-grade class science experiment, I never had a pet chicken. But most of us can probably imagine this picture of a mother hen protecting her chicks. Her instinct to shield her babies from harm is just as ingrained into who she is, as it is an inseparable aspect of who God is. What chick in its right mind would run from such a sure and comforting shelter?

One of the greatest lessons I have learned from my pets is how to trust and not worry when you have an "owner" who truly loves and cares for you. Even on my most stressful days, I could always look over at any one of my pets and see them resting peacefully. They knew I would care for their needs.

[64]Psalm 61:4
[65]Matthew 23:37

Jesus taught His disciples not to worry about this life — such as their possessions, and having enough to eat or clothes to wear. Humans, especially in the western world, certainly have a way of letting those things consume us, don't we? In fact, we worry so much about them that we lose sight of eternal things. We create within our lives a vicious cycle of trying to survive, and striving to thrive. We believe if we prepare enough, work hard enough, that we'll be ready for anything!

However, I think we need to allow ourselves to experience hurt and sadness, which will doubtless come at some point for all of us. A state of depression fine-tunes our senses and our hearts. When we feel the difficulty of simply putting one foot in front of the other, we understand how much we need help. We finally have eyes to see that God was always there, ready to supply us with whatever we need, and to comfort and protect us in whatever we face.

"Consider the ravens," Jesus said. *"They do not sow or reap. They have no storeroom or barn; yet God feeds them."*[66]

"Consider how the lilies grow," he added. *"They do not labor or spin. Yet I tell you, not even Solomon in all his splendor was dressed like one of these."*[67]

If God cares that much for the wild birds and flowers, He certainly cares for you. Creation knows that. Your pet knew that. You just need to know that.

After we lost Max, a dear friend called me to express her condolences. She also took the time to share about the loss of a dog she once had many years ago. Her story was heartbreaking. As a little girl, she had longed for a puppy. She finally got one for Christmas, and she dearly loved that puppy, which she named Princess, and formed a deep bond

[66]Luke 12:24
[67]Luke 12:27

with her. But when it came time for her to go to school full-time, her parents decided to give the dog away to an uncle, as they would not have the time to care for her anymore. My friend was heartbroken, but she was told she would be able to visit the dog from time to time. Not long after this, however, she got devastating news that the puppy had run away. They never found her.

Though her family over the years took in other dogs, my friend told me that she never really loved the others like she loved her Princess.

"I loved my first," she said. "Princess would always be the love of my life."

Especially having experienced this tragedy at such a young age, this memory left a lasting impression on my friend, which continues to this day, decades later. She still has sadness and wonders what happened to her sweet little puppy. But she also has a great faith in God, and has learned to navigate her grief. She has experienced His peace in her life, which has given her purpose to keep moving on. She has learned to leave everything – her past, present and future – in His capable, loving hands. And she finds comfort in believing that when she goes to heaven, she'll find Princess there.

In your exhausting, prolonged sadness, know that there is always One who will take care of you. You are not alone. He validates your depression, but He does not want you to stay there forever. He will use this time to heal you and empower you to keep moving and to eventually find peace and victory in His wonderful plan.

"My comfort in my suffering is this: Your promise preserves my life."[68]

---

[68]Psalm 119:50

Prayer

Dear Father,

The reality of _____'s passing is hitting me so hard. I feel a deep sense of loss, knowing that (he/she) is not coming back. _____ filled my heart and my home in so many ways, and now life seems so empty, even purposeless. I grieve because I lost my best friend. I groan with all of creation for a day when this kind of pain and sadness ceases. Help me to allow the depression to hone my hope. Bring me comfort as I mourn. I need the Holy Spirit to intercede for me in my weakness. Thank you that you're working out a plan for ultimate good, and that in this world so full of commotion you are my Rock that I can always depend on. Help me to rely on you, just as the ravens and lilies do, for your abundant provision. Thank you for your promises of comfort and protection, especially during this time of great heartache. As I take shelter under your wings, please transform my sorrow to assurance in your promise of new life for me and for all of your beloved creation.

In Jesus' Name, Amen

Chapter 5

When You Want to Live Again but Don't Know How

Chance was a stray who wandered into our family at just the right time. Several years before, we had lost our dog Snooper, a beagle/collie mix. Snooper is the family dog I remember most during my childhood years; we lost him to cancer when he was 12. About a month before Chance came, we tragically lost another dog, Sparky, when he got loose and was struck by a hit and run driver. Each loss, one being expected and one so sudden, resulted in different kinds of grief that had to be navigated.

Chance's name suited him in more ways than one. We gave him a chance for a safe and loving home, and he gave us a chance to heal and love again. This black lab mutt was my best friend for all of my 20s. That decade brought a lot of soul-searching and changes for me, but he was always there to cheer me up with a snuggle, and to get me out of the house for exercise of both body and soul. He was my buddy.

Sadly, in 2012, after about 10 years with him, our family made the difficult decision to say a sorrowful goodbye to him. He had suffered a stroke and was most likely to suffer another one any day, far worse and possibly fatal. That same year, my cat Alley and my chinchilla Moses, both at their life expectancy, also passed away. It was also the year I got married and started a new chapter in my life. At that point, it is almost as if they all fulfilled their purpose of being my companions, and now could enter their rest as I was entering a new phase of life. The timing seemed more than simple coincidence.

We love our pets. We never have enough time with them. But the reality is that we will most likely outlive most of them. We will lose them in one way or another. Age and disease will set in, or sometimes accidents happen. The reality does not make grief any easier. But it does mean that we will need to find a way to keep living. And I think our pets would want us to live well and not be consumed with sadness. That is the best way to honor them, after all. Getting to that point, however, cannot be rushed. There is no timetable.

Accepting your pet's passing does not mean that you are suddenly cured of grief. We just learn to grieve in a healthier manner, for the long-term. That means we do not just settle in for an excruciating existence of sad resignation. We look to the past for treasures to hold on to, and we look to the future with a great hope, beyond our wildest imaginations- a future that is built on the sure promises of God.

Find closure

Accepting your pet's passing does not at all mean that your pet is ever forgotten. Sometimes, when we get to a place where the sadness doesn't feel so intense, we start to feel guilty for moving on without them. But I believe it is possible, and necessary, to be sad without being crippled by depression, or guilt, or mentally rehashing their last moments. They were more than their final hours, minutes, or seconds, much more.

I believe an important part of moving on, then, is to ensure that your heart is in a place where you are ready to honor your pet's amazing memory. When you find freedom from the cycle of intense grief, you can live again – and perhaps with renewed purpose from the lessons your pet taught you. When you find closure, a deep and abiding joy can commence, because the memories are no longer marred by misery, but are garnished with gratitude.

First, it is important that you express everything that is on your mind. Say whatever you need to, admit where you still struggle. Share both your negative and positive thoughts to God and to others in your life who understand. If you need to write a letter to your pet, saying everything you want to say, then do that. Don't allow anything to go unresolved. God's Word says that He hears and answers His people when we cry out to Him to set us free from our sorrows: *"The righteous cry out, and the LORD hears them; he delivers them from all their troubles. The LORD is close to the brokenhearted and saves those who are crushed in spirit."*[69]

Second, discover creative ways to remember and honor your pet. My sister-in-law blessed us with beautiful, personalized plaques after both Howie's and Max's passing. We have them displayed along with their cremation boxes and pawprints. I bought a shadowbox to display photos of Max, his pawprints, collar, and some of his fur. Before Max's passing, I wrote a children's book about him, which we hope to publish soon as a way to continue sharing his fun and smart personality with others, as well as to pass on an important lesson about love that he taught us. What are some ways you can honor the unique gift that your pet was to you and the world?

Third, and related to that, be thankful to God for the time you had with your pet. God chose to bless you both with each other. Our pets probably blessed us more than we could ever have blessed them. Since the beginning of time, God used the animals to teach us important lessons. Elijah learned of obedience and trust in God's provision through ravens (1

Kings 17:1-6). Balaam learned of God's power and sovereignty through a talking donkey (Numbers 22:21-35)! Often, the animals' sweet, loyal love provides a glimpse into God's love for us, too. Sometimes sharing your pet's story and the lessons they taught you is a great way to remember them and to keep them alive, not just in your own heart, but to keep passing on the blessing that they were to others.

My oldest sister and her family moved to a farm in Texas several years ago. There, one of my nieces was able to fuel her growing love for horses and the growing sense of a divine call to serve both God and people by working with them. At that time, Coco, a bay Quarter Horse mare, came into her life.

"She was older and brought more emotional and physical baggage with her than I could even understand at that time," she said. "Nonetheless, she gave her whole heart and had the kindest spirit; essentially, she was the perfect first horse for a girl who needed to learn about compassion and unconditional love."

And then the day before Thanksgiving in 2021, Coco was unable to recover from a severe case of impaction colic.

"Losing her was one of the hardest things I've ever experienced," she said, "and the months that followed were filled with waves of intense grief." My niece was grateful for the many friends who reached out to her with condolences and comforting Scripture. She also found comfort in knowing that Coco's legacy would not be forgotten.

"Even in the painful moments where I had to come to grips with the fact that my best friend was gone, I felt a peace in knowing that she had impacted my life and changed my heart to such an extent where her legacy will undoubtedly live on."

It was because of Coco that my niece developed the confidence to intern with a professional horse trainer, to start teaching horsemanship lessons, and to continue growing as an equestrian so she can help other horses and people even more.

"In a way, she was a true godsend, and I often tell people how God knew I needed horses so He could speak through them to my heart," she said, adding, "I genuinely feel that without Coco, I would be a completely different person today. She was a light in my life, and she gave me the courage to step out of my comfort zone so that I might share some of that light with the world."

My niece discovered her very calling with the help of Coco. She continues to honor both God and Coco with the lessons she taught her. I have no doubt Coco's legacy is written in permanent ink on my niece's heart and the hearts of countless others who have been and will be touched by the precious gift that she was.

Fourth and finally, we can find closure in recognizing the "good" in "good-bye." In his book, Wright offers important, encouraging etymology to this oft-used phrase: "The word *good-bye* – originally 'God be with you' or 'Go with God' – was a recognition that God was a significant part of the going. Perhaps we have forgotten that along with the journey we gain strength when we remember that the Giver of life is there to protect and console, especially when the good-bye is because of death."[70] Perhaps when you start to feel as though you need to find a way to begin living again after your pet's passing, you can say aloud to your pet, even if it's a gentle whisper: *"Go with God."* There are no safer hands for them to be in. They ran their race, and they finished well. After Max's

[70]H. Norman Wright, *Experiencing Grief* (Nashville, Tennessee: B&H Publishing Group, 2004), 75.

passing, my mom astutely observed that he and Maya seemed to have lived more in their short 10 years than we as people do in 80. I think we need to follow our pet's example and finish well with whatever years we are given, until it is time for us to "go with God" too, to our final reward.

Look to the future

For several weeks after Max's passing, I couldn't bear to go downstairs or in the backyard. It was hard enough being other places in the house without him there, but those were the areas that held the most memories. It was too painful. I was too much in shock. But even as I avoided certain areas, I couldn't avoid the crushing emptiness of the house that his loss left behind.

Several weeks passed. Having grown up with rescue pets and having volunteered with dog rescue organizations, I was well aware of the many critters out there always in need of a loving home. We had fostered dogs in the past, so we tentatively began looking into some rescues that might have a dog that would suit our situation. I was specifically looking for an older dog, since they are often overlooked. I wanted to have a purpose in the connection. I felt helping a dog truly in need would get my mind focused on something other than my heartache. I felt that it would also help me to justify bringing another dog into what was "Max's house" for so many years. I had to deal with the guilty feelings surrounding such a move, so it was difficult to say the least.

That's how we met Bailey, an approximately 10-year-old black and white pit bull/lab mix. A local rescue sent us her picture and said she was being housed at a nearby kennel after her owner, who had adopted her for about a year, was dealing with severe health issues and could no longer care for her. She apparently had a rough life before meeting him. The first time she had arrived at the rescue she was pregnant. All of her puppies died except one. The puppy found a loving home, and so did Bailey. When I learned her story and realized her last owner had no choice but to surrender her, I immediately thought of how much we had in common. Bailey had just lost her best friend, and we had just lost ours. We needed each other.

As soon as she came into our home, she was a perfect angel. She was obedient, compliant, and gave the sweetest snuggles. I really believe God led us to her. He knew we needed her. She helped us to heal. Max's loss hit us hard, and we still think of him and grieve for him often. But she helped us to keep moving.

Not everyone will follow that same path. Perhaps getting another pet is something that will help you. Perhaps you need more time. Perhaps that will never be something that you will do. But no matter what your future entails, it is important to keep pressing on and embracing the path, the race, still marked out for you.

Satan and his minions want us to remain in the dark of hopelessness. Jesus told us in no uncertain terms, *"The thief [Satan] comes only to steal and kill and destroy..."*[71] In contrast, Jesus said of Himself, *"I have come that they may have life, and have it to the full."*[72] God is described as wrapping Himself in light as with a garment (Psalm 104:2). Jesus, God in flesh, announced that He was the Light of the world (John 8:12), who came to point the world back to God: *"I have come into the world as a light, so that no one who believes in me should stay in*

[71]John 10:10a
[72]John 10:10b

darkness."[73] We must recognize that there *is* an unseen, super-
natural battle raging that threatens to steal our hope, to cause
us pain. But we can also have sure faith that the light always
is more powerful than darkness: *"The light shines in the darkness,
and the darkness has not overcome it."*[74] God, through Jesus Christ,
has offered us freedom and restoration even now, and will one
day fully restore all that is broken. It is looking to that day, not
just today in its feelings of loss and sadness, that can give us
the strength to keep going, and to do so even with unexplain-
able joy.

In his seminal work, *Mere Christianity*, C.S. Lewis wrote,
"If I find in myself desires which nothing in this world can
satisfy, the only logical explanation is that I was made for
another world."[75] Loss and pain is evidence that this is not our
home. Such experiences are foreign to our sense of right and
good. Though we live in a fallen world, we are still marked –
albeit compromised at times by our sin and rebelliousness – by
the image of God. Grief is unnatural to that original design.
We long for grief to end, and we long for something better to
take its place.

Redemption calls us back to how things were always
intended to be, and reminds us that we were meant for something better. All is not lost! Such perspective, however, is
something humanity has struggled to fathom since the beginning of time. We find ourselves stuck in the mire of trials and
tribulations over and over again, grasping desperately at what

[73]John 12:46

[74]John 1:5, Holy Bible, New International Version®, NIV® Copyright
©1973, 1978, 1984, 2011 by Biblica, Inc.® Used by permission. All rights
reserved worldwide.

[75]C.S. Lewis, *Mere Christianity* (New York, New York: HarperOne, 1980),
136-137.

we pray are glimmers of hope. But we don't have to grasp at all. Jesus Christ came to definitively show that hope has come. It is present and tangible, and far better than we could devise in our own minds.

In the account of Lazarus's death in John 11, there is a lot of grieving going on. Lazarus and his sisters, Mary and Martha, were friends with Jesus. They would have been well aware of Jesus's ability to heal. He had healed so many among the crowds that followed Him and the people He met as he traveled from city to city. That is why when Lazarus fell ill, Mary and Martha sent word to Jesus to come right away. But He delayed. On purpose. He waited until Lazarus was good and dead for several days before He came. Why?

When Jesus first heard that Lazarus was sick, He told His disciples that his sickness would not end in death (John 11:4). But there he was, dead. When Jesus arrived at their home, Martha said to Jesus, *"Lord...if you had been here, my brother would not have died."*[76] Mary came to Jesus later and said the same thing (John 11:32). But Jesus wanted them to know that preventing death was not necessarily the only way that God worked.

Granted, Martha did believe in God's promise of an end-of-days resurrection, when all who died would rise again to new and eternal life. She even believed that Jesus was the Christ, the Messiah, the promised one of God who came into the world to save it. But her brother's life in this world? It was over, in her mind.

But Jesus challenged her thinking: *"I am the resurrection and the life. He who believes in me will live, even though he dies; and whoever lives and believes in me will never die. Do you believe this?"*[77]

[76]John 11:21
[77]John 11:25-26

Later, Jesus looked around and saw Mary and a crowd around her weeping over Lazarus's death. Jesus was *"deeply moved in spirit and troubled,"* and he wept too.[78] I think Jesus's response is multifaceted.

First, I do not believe Jesus grieved because Lazarus had died. He knew that that was not going to be the end. In fact, He knew this entire scenario was happening so that He could show them, beyond a shadow of any doubt, who He really was as their Messiah.

Second, I believe He did grieve with the crowd because He understood the pain they were feeling, just as He understands the pain that you are feeling with the loss that you experienced. He was fully God yet also fully man, and He was sensitive to the heartache that we experience in this world where sickness and death are agonizing realities.

But third, and most importantly, I believe Jesus's deepest grief was due to the lack of understanding by the crowd as to who He was. Even those intimately acquainted with Him and His miracles still lacked the faith to see His true mission and His true power. The crowd thought that Jesus was crying simply because he loved Lazarus. Others wondered, *"Could not he who opened the eyes of the blind man have kept this man from dying?"*[79]

Those responses led Jesus to be even more deeply moved by their lack of faith. But you know what else was moved that day? The stone that had been rolled in front of Lazarus's tomb. At Jesus's command, Lazarus came out of the tomb, and Jesus ordered those around him to take off his grave clothes.

Jesus made it clear that He performed this miracle to show the crowds the glory of God (John 11:40). He showed

[78]John 11:33, 35
[79]John 11:37

them that He was not to be placed in a box of their limited understanding or beliefs. That is a lesson we still need to take with us today. Our hope in Jesus Christ as the resurrection and the life must supersede our often-limited expectations that lead to nothing more than a resignation toward disappointment, discouragement, and depression.

Do you have that hope? Have you come to know Jesus for who He really is?

Jesus shares in your grief and went to the greatest length to free you from despair and to secure a future that makes these momentary troubles seem so very small. In fact, our current pain and loss only prepares us for, and reminds us of, better things to come. *"For our light and momentary troubles are achieving for us an eternal glory that far outweighs them all."*[80] If you put your faith and trust in Jesus, there is a new work happening in you and for you that you cannot see with your eyes: *"Though outwardly we are wasting away, yet inwardly we are being renewed day by day."*[81] You are empowered to face everything in this life, even the greatest suffering: *"And the God of all grace, who called you to his eternal glory in Christ, after you have suffered a little while, will himself restore you and make you strong, firm and steadfast."*[82]

When we hide ourselves in Jesus, we can trade anxiety for anticipation. We can trade our heartache for hope. He defeated death when he rose from the grave, and there is coming a day when death will be destroyed completely (1 Corinthians 15:26). And then will come what we have *all* been waiting for.

[80] 2 Corinthians 4:17
[81] 2 Corinthians 4:16
[82] 1 Peter 5:10

"He [Jesus Christ] must remain in heaven until the time comes for God to restore everything, as he promised long ago through his holy prophets."[83]

"Restoration" has a beautiful ring to it, doesn't it? All that is broken will be made brand new. All that has been lost will be found again, and made better than ever – eternal. On that day, in the new heaven and new earth, *"He will wipe every tear from [our] eyes. There will be no more death or mourning or crying or pain, for the old order of things has passed away."*[84]

As you seek to live again, you will no doubt have to learn to live with the emptiness that your pet's loss has left behind. But I pray that the hope that lies ahead, for those who trust in Jesus for salvation and restoration, will make you strong and purposeful in all your remaining days here on earth.

[83]Acts 3:21
[84]Revelation 21:4

Prayer

Dear Father,

Thank you for the gift of _____. He/she brought me so much joy, comfort, and companionship. I know that he/she is gone. I accept that fact, but I still don't know how I'm going to keep going on here without him/her. He/she showed me so much love. He/she was a part of my daily routine, and my life was richer with him/her in it. He/she was my best friend, and I think I will always grieve this profound, heartbreaking loss. Help me to know how to honor their memory in the best way possible, and to use what they taught me about love and life to bless others. Thank you that I can know that _____ is safe, because he/she is in your hands. Thank you also that you have blessed us with the Lord Jesus, through whom we can have an eternal future that transcends all the pain and loss that we experience in this temporary life and world. Thank you that you are with me in my suffering, and that one day that suffering will end completely. Help me to stay faithful, always full of hope. Give me strength to continue trusting, serving, and loving. I hold on to the promise that grief will not be the last word.

In Jesus' Name, Amen.

Chapter 6

Will I See My Pet Again?

When it comes to the topic of heaven and an afterlife, one of the most frequently asked questions is if we will see our beloved best friends again.

It is the most natural desire for those of us who love our pets so much. We want to have hope that one day we will experience a joyful reunion with them. We want to know that our "good-bye" was only a "see you later."

Many theories have been proposed over the years in an effort to prove that our pets are not gone forever. Some believe their pet continues to abide with them in a spiritual state or visit them in dreams. Others believe they can contact their deceased pet via a pet medium. Many more hold onto the hope that we'll all eventually be together again in heaven.

As I mentioned at the start of this book, my goal in writing all of this has been to validate your grief and present you with a path from grief to joy. I have walked this path ahead of you, but I did not mark it out. I was guided by God's Word. He is the sole Creator of the universe, who set all things into motion and is continually, intimately aware of every detail, so I honestly do not know how we can turn anywhere else. Jesus, who is described in Scripture as the Word that became flesh (John 1:14), stated in no uncertain terms that He is the way, the truth, and the life (John 14:6). He is our one and only connection to heaven.

The way I see it, it is much easier to know that our hope lies in our Creator, the transcendent God, than to try to find hope in theories or ideas that are really nothing more than vapor. As good as they sound, the truth is far better – not just because it is true but because it is based on a faithful, compassionate God who dearly loves all that His hands have made.

With that foundation, let me share with you what I believe to be the answer to the question, "Will I see my pet again?" I pray it leads you to the same assurance and peace that I have obtained.

Is there a "Rainbow Bridge"?

"The Rainbow Bridge" has become a popular poem used to give comfort to bereaved pet owners. It speaks of a special place where our deceased pets go. Those animals that shared a special bond with their human go to this beautiful place where they experience restored health, joy, companionship, and all the blessings an animal could ever want. Except, they miss the beloved human(s) they left behind. The poem ends with the anticipation of a day when the owner arrives, they have a joyous reunion, and then they cross the rainbow bridge together.

The poem describes everything our hurting hearts could wish for. Our best friends are happy and healed and not gone from our lives forever. Who doesn't want to believe that?

As beautiful as the poem is, we must recognize that it is just one author's poetic description of the hope they had. It is not something to build a belief upon. However, if we take that poem and compare it with what the Bible says – in which we *can* find truth – could such a place be a possibility?

In His Word, God does not explicitly lay out for us the future plans He has for the animals. There is no mention of a "Rainbow Bridge." But I believe there are concepts in Scripture that can give us peace about our pets, and even suggest that reunification with them is not as far-fetched as it might sound to some. But first, it is what the Bible *doesn't* say that can give us reason to hope. The Bible does not deny the possibility of a reunification with our pets. In fact, there seems to be more evidence pointing *toward* this hope than away from it.

Throughout this book, I have already shared truths found in the Bible regarding God's care for the animals. He created each of them and continues to watch over them. He gave humans the responsibility of watching over them as well. I shared previously that God sees and honors the bonds that we make with special animals that come into our lives. I tend to believe that at the very least God will once again, perhaps at the final resurrection and in the new heaven and the new earth, bless us with a reunion with the animals that brought us so much happiness on this earth. He certainly is able. Phillips and Hastings write, "Who is to say that a creature which has become the loyal friend of a human being, will not be there, in the presence of God with whom all things are possible?"[85]

In addition, we know from Romans 8 that all of creation groans and awaits restoration. Many well-meaning Christians argue that because animals do not have souls or the ability to repent of their sins and accept Jesus Christ as Savior, that they will not be in heaven. Without getting too far into the theological weeds, I would simply counter that animals also never had free will to sin, and therefore never sinned and do not need to secure salvation. If they do not have souls, we do know they were directly formed by God's own loving hand (Genesis 2:19). I have a hard time believing that He would

---

[85]John Phillips and Jim Hastings, *Exploring Ecclesiastes: An Expository Commentary* (Grand Rapids, Michigan: Kregel Publications, 2019), 136.

just cast them aside forever. He is ever seeking to save. In fact, the psalmist wrote, *"O LORD, you preserve both man and beast."*[86]

In Ecclesiastes 3:20-21, the "Preacher" is wondering aloud whether the fate of men and animals is the same: *"All go to the same place; all come from dust, and to dust all return. Who knows if the spirit of man rises upward and if the spirit of the animal goes down into the earth?"*

Ecclesiastes is often attributed to Solomon, and if so, then this book is written by the wisest man ever known to live. Yet even he could only surmise where the spirits of both man and animal go when they die. Eternity is beyond our understanding. Yet when Jesus came from heaven to earth to bring the message of God's Kingdom to us, He gave us a better glimpse. He gave us greater insight into the redemption plan of Almighty God. Regarding the fate of animals, Phillips and Hastings write, "Certainly, we cannot dogmatize but wouldn't that be just like Jesus, to give us back our faithful, humble friends in that land of fadeless day?"[87]

God is able to do anything. God is love. He cares for the animals better than we ever could. That sure truth is greater than any pie in the sky hope for a mythical place devised in our limited human minds. We do not have to guess or wish. We can know. We can trust that He will do what is best.

Where our hope is found

If our pets do go to heaven when they die, or if they will be resurrected to live in the new heaven and the new earth, that does not automatically mean that we will be reunited with

---

[86]Psalm 36:6
[87]Phillips and Hastings, 137

them. Why? Because that only answers the question of what happens to *them*. It does not answer what will happen to *you*. You have to make sure that is where *you* will be one day.

It is because of grace through Jesus Christ that we can be saved from the sin that keeps us in darkness in this world. It is because of Jesus Christ that we can have the hope of a home in heaven, and for all things to be restored in the end. Therefore, it is only if we are found in Him that we can have the hope of possibly seeing our pets, or other loved ones for that matter, when our time on earth is over.

"For the wages of sin is death, but the gift of God is eternal life in Christ Jesus our Lord."[88]

Eternal life comes only through Christ. Many want to think good thoughts about going to heaven. But thoughts don't get you there. Only a relationship with Christ can do that. He extended grace to us. All we have to do is take hold of it. Our only peace and hope, in this life and the next, is found in Christ.

In Christ. Those are key words. They remind us where our focus should be – *on whom* our focus should be. If we have a desire to go to heaven, but deny Christ, that desire will never be realized. If we only want to go to heaven because we may get to see our beloved pet again, our focus is blurred and we lose the peace and joy that comes only through Christ. In a sense, we are dishonoring our pet, and God, by making him or her into an idol.

Our hope, happiness and joy does not rest in the good things – such as our pets – around us, but in the Creator who made all things good. From Him came and comes all life, all good things. In fact, He gives nothing *but* good: *"Every good and*

---

[88]Romans 6:23

perfect gift is from above, coming down from the Father of the heavenly lights, who does not change like shifting shadows."[89]

Outside of God, there is only darkness and hopelessness. God is the source of light. He needs to be our primary focus: *"Whom have I in heaven but you? And earth has nothing I desire besides you. My flesh and my heart may fail, but God is the strength of my heart and my portion forever."*[90]

We are created for worship – for worshiping the one and only God who sent Jesus, who died, rose again, providing for our salvation. Our compassionate Creator has more planned for us than we could ever imagine. He breathed life into our pets in the first place. He is the reason we had the chance to know and enjoy them at all. They are the good things that come from our good God. Worship Him, and find hope in Him alone.

When we have received salvation and allow the Holy Spirit to give us this right, humble attitude toward God, we can have a beautiful communion with Him in which we can ask Him for anything. We can talk to Him about anything. We can talk to Him about all our fears, our hurts, our hopes, and our dreams. He teaches us more about Himself, and we grow in the beauty and power of His loving embrace. So, if you want to ask Him about your beloved pet, go ahead and ask. If you want to ask Him for the blessing of seeing your pet again in heaven, go ahead and ask. He loves to give good gifts to His children, to bless them extravagantly. Perhaps He is just waiting for us to ask Him, rather than to debate or wish or conjure up our own ideas about what happens in the afterlife.

[89]James 1:17
[90]Psalm 73:25-26

When we meet with Him and talk with Him, He has a powerful and effective way of meeting with us, giving us peace, and filling our hearts with excitement about what is to come. When our focus is on loving and thanking God, we can find peace and rest in knowing that everything will fall into place according to His good and perfect plan. Let Him transform you in the present and prepare you for the beautiful future that is ahead. A future that will be far beyond what we could ever hope for, and may just include our beloved best friends.

"No eye has seen, no ear has heard, no mind has conceived what God has prepared for those who love him."[91]

---

[91] 1 Corinthians 2:9; Isaiah 64:4

Prayer

Dear Father,

I would love to see my pet again. It brings me peace to know that it is a possibility. Help me to leave the future in your loving and capable hands. I trust in Jesus Christ for salvation from my sin, and for the future restoration of this decaying world. Thank you for the hope we have in Him. I can't wait for Heaven. I don't know exactly what eternity will look like, but I know it will be the best place I or my pet could ever go. Everything You do is good, and You can only give gifts that are good. I trust You, and more than I want to see anything else, I want to see You.

"Now to him who is able to do immeasurably more than all we ask or imagine, according to his power that is at work within us, to him be glory in the church and in Christ Jesus throughout all generations, for ever and ever! Amen."[92]

[92]Ephesians 3:20-21

Bibliography

Allison, D.C. Jr. *Matthew: Volume 1:1-7.* International Critical Commentary. London: Bloomsbury T&T Clark, 2004.

Blue, Debbie. *Consider the Birds: A Provocative Guide to Birds of the Bible.* Nashville, Tennessee: Abingdon Press, 2013.

Fogal, John W. Sr. *Living the Beatitudes: See how you are being conformed to the image of Christ.* ChurchSmart Resources, 2013.

Gane, Roy. *Old Testament Law for Christians: Original context and enduring application.* Grand Rapids, Michigan: Baker Academic, 2017.

Lewis, C.S. *Mere Christianity.* New York, New York: HarperOne, 1980.

Morris, Leon. *The Epistle to the Romans.* Grand Rapids, Michigan: William B. Eerdmans Publishing Company, 1988.

Phillips, John and Jim Hastings. *Exploring Ecclesiastes: An Expository Commentary.* Grand Rapids, Michigan: Kregel Publications, 2019.

Waltke, Bruce K. and Cathi J. Fredricks. *Genesis: A Commentary.* Grand Rapids, Michigan: Zondervan, 2001.

Wright, H. Norman. *Experiencing Grief.* Nashville, Tennessee: B&H Publishing Group, 2004.

Author Bio

Tricia Kline is the president of Extra Second, Inc. An award-winning journalist and author of several fiction and non-fiction books, she is also a Bible teacher and professor and is currently pursuing a PhD in Bible exposition. She lives in central Pennsylvania with her husband and rescue pets. For more information, visit www.extrasecond.com.

Pet Tributes

Marley and Codi. Miss you two every day. You were the best boys ever!

Chicky. I rescued Chiquitin (Chicky) last year and the Lord blessed me with a new buddy. A senior dog, he left me in September. ~ David Rundle

Rascal. You were clever, lovable, and would do anything to be part of the crew. Fifteen years was not long enough. You are missed dearly, Rascal. ~ The Kline family (Ben, RuthAnn, Justin, Josh, Becky, and Rachel).

Benjamin (Benny, Ben, Pupstar, Benji) Rupert Nissly (2009–2021). Benny Nissly was family and a best friend. He was a very good and faithful dog. We loved him well and will never forget him. ~Ryan, Lori, Gabriel, Levi, Jacob, and Aaron Nissly

Shadow. You were such a happy, loving family dog. We miss you every day, especially your constant requests for a belly rub. We love you sweet girl! ~ The Peters family (Mike, Lori, Sarah and Jenna).

Made in United States
North Haven, CT
20 September 2023

41781125R00055